STUDY SKILLS
STRATEGIES:
ACCELERATE YOUR LEARNING

Uelaine A. Lengefeld

CRISP PUBLICATIONS, INC.
Menlo Park, California

WARNING:

FAILURE TO USE THE TECHNIQUES IN THIS BOOK COULD BE HAZARDOUS TO YOUR G.P.A.

CREDITS
Editor: **Michael G. Crisp**
Layout & Composition: **Interface Studio**
Cover Design: **Carol Harris**
Artwork: **Ralph Mapson**

Copyright © 1986, 1987, 1994 by Crisp Publications, Inc.
Printed in the United States of America

English language Crisp books are distributed worldwide. Our major international distributors include:

CANADA: Reid Publishing Ltd., Box 69559—109 Thomas St., Oakville, Ontario, Canada L6J 7R4. TEL: (905) 842-4428, FAX: (905) 842-9327

Raincoast Books Distribution Ltd., 112 East 3rd Avenue, Vancouver, British Columbia, Canada V5T 1C8. TEL: (604) 873-6581, FAX: (604) 874-2711

AUSTRALIA: Career Builders, P.O. Box 1051, Springwood, Brisbane, Queensland, Australia 4127. TEL: 841-1061, FAX: 841-1580

NEW ZEALAND: Career Builders, P.O. Box 571, Manurewa, Auckland, New Zealand. TEL: 266-5276, FAX: 266-4152

JAPAN: Phoenix Associates Co., Mizuho Bldg. 2-12-2, Kami Osaki, Shinagawa-Ku, Tokyo 141, Japan. TEL: 3-443-7231, FAX: 3-443-7640

Selected Crisp titles are also available in other languages. Contact International Rights Manager Suzanne Kelly at (415) 323-6100 for more information.

Library of Congress Catalog Card Number 93-074051
Lengefeld, Uelaine
Study Skills Strategies: Accelerate Your Learning
ISBN 1-56052-260-7

This book is printed on recyclable paper with soy ink.

PRINTED WITH SOY INK

PREFACE

This book is a thorough revision of the extremely successful STUDY SKILLS STRATEGIES (1987). In order to accelerate your learning, this edition contains the newest research on the way we process information in the brain, plus a new section on the role affirmations can play in reprogramming our thinking. Adult learners and students of all ages can profit from the additional memory techniques contained in this addition.

A vast majority of students do not learn effective study skills. As a result, they never achieve their potential in an academic program. For academic advisors, retention and support programs, orientation staff, and students, STUDY SKILLS STRATEGIES is a refreshing, time-saving, and inexpensive method to acquire quality study skills.

The learning strategies in this module are flexible. For example, this book can be used in summer or weekend college preparatory sessions; one unit credit classes offered by Learning Resource Centers; high school study skills programs; freshman orientation classes; workshops for re-entry students; or by any adult needing to learn new skills.

Also, transfer programs at the college level have successfully incorporated these materials into a university transition program, and EOP programs have used the book with special admissions students. Finally, tutor training programs will find the "checklist for tutors and instructors" on page 87 useful.

When a student reaches out for help, a comprehensive, theoretical book is overwhelming. Thanks to the brevity and readability of this manual, students react positively. Even without a formal class, students can make progress thanks to the self-study format.

We have made every effort to keep STUDY SKILLS STRATEGIES simple and practical so readers will keep it as a quick reference to refresh their skills as the need arises.

TO THE INSTRUCTOR

INSTRUCTIONAL SUGGESTIONS

Sections I-VII of this book can be used in a variety of ways. For example, the material can be the basis for weekly study skills assignments. Also, learning strategies group leaders can apply units to content-specific assignments. Individual tutors will find sections managable, and learning resource centers like the self-paced format for individualized instruction plans. It is also ideal for tutor training programs, and the checklist in APPENDIX II has been used effectively in the Instructional Support Center at California State Polytechnic University, Pomona.

All *basic* Study Skills sections contain alternative coaching strategies. These allow the student to practice the application of a particular skill. It is suggested an approach be used which requires students to apply previous skills, rather than teaching isolated units without relating them to the other study elements.

''Learning Ladders'' have been included throughout the book to reinforce the idea that learning must be an active process. These were designed to give students an extra learning boost.

TO THE READER

Fear of the unknown is both normal and healthy. It can be a powerful motivator. On the other hand, too much fear can cause procrastination, and in some cases, paralysis. If you learn proven study skills strategies much of the fear about college, or any new learning experience, will fade.

Your anxiety will diminish and your confidence will grow once you are familiar with the study skills in this book that were designed to help you accomplish the following objectives:

1. Learning to analyze your attitudes toward studying and your current study skills habits.

2. Achieving a sense of personal power, thanks to the time management and goal setting exercises you will complete.

3. Taking clear, meaningful classroom notes and learning how to study from them.

4. Developing power reading skills such as SQ3R which will teach you to systematically mark and take study notes on a college level textbook.

5. Acquiring better methods to memorize material for long term recall.

6. Developing organizational patterns which will help you use imagery to visualize concepts and encode new material.

7. Learning how to prepare for and take objective exams.

8. Understanding the techniques which will assist you to write better essays.

9. Using study aids and oral recitation to improve your performance on tests.

10. Making a commitment to practice new study skills strategies by completing a learning contract APPENDIX I.

All of these objectives can be achieved. It will take effort on your part, but if you are serious about your studies, it will be well worth the time you invest.

I welcome correspondence from you about these or *other* successful strategies you use so they can be shared with students struggling to find an easier way.

Your Learning Strategies Coach,

Uelaine A. Lengefeld

ACKNOWLEDGEMENTS

Special thanks go to Elwood Chapman for his ideas and for his special mentoring throughout the creation of the first edition. Without Mr. Chapman and the assistance of Tonie Lynne Kennedy, the book would never have come to fruition. Michael Crisp's talented editorial pen was essential, and I am grateful for his original assistance.

I also want to acknowledge Professors Walter Pauk, Lilian Metlitzky, Martha Maxwell, Frank Robinson, Frank Christ, and Colin Rose for research contributions in the field of learning and reading skills.

Finally, this book is dedicated to Lorraine Wall, my mother, and Katherine Lengefeld, my daughter, because they have always believed in me and my dreams.

CONTENTS

PART

I

GETTING STARTED

YOUR ATTITUDE
TOWARD STUDYING

This section of STUDY SKILLS STRATEGIES was designed to help you know yourself better. The exercises and self-assessments are for your personal information. There are no right answers—but for this program to be effective, you must be honest with yourself.

Throughout the book you will find boxes called "Learning Ladders." These will help you practice and apply some of the more important concepts that have been presented.

DISCOVER YOUR ATTITUDE TOWARD LEARNING

To learn and apply quality study skills, it is essential to have a positive attitude. In fact, your attitude and motivation will make all the difference. To measure your attitude toward studying, complete this exercise. If the statement describes your attitude or study habit check *YES* and if not check *NO*. *Be very honest.*

ATTITUDES	YES	NO
1. I am satisfied with my test scores on most examinations.	☐	☐
2. If I do poorly on a test, I increase my efforts and get help from a teacher, a tutor, or a study partner.	☐	☐
3. When required, I can concentrate on studies. I am not easily distracted.	☐	☐
4. The challenge of taking study notes on difficult textbook reading does not throw me.	☐	☐
5. Although busy, I am able to find priority time to study. Procrastination and cramming are not problems for me.	☐	☐
6. I attend class regularly and carefully prepare for most class sessions.	☐	☐
7. I have a clear reason for going to school and know that good study skills will get me closer to my career goal.	☐	☐
8. When I have a boring instructor, I realize I must work harder to make the material interesting.	☐	☐
9. My moods or personal problems seldom prevent me from completing my work.	☐	☐
10. I can visualize myself completing my goal.	☐	☐
11. I know how to reward myself for finishing a difficult assignment.	☐	☐
12. I listen carefully while taking class notes, and I review them within 24 hours.	☐	☐

For any item where you checked NO, be sure to carefully read the section of this book devoted to that particular study skill. This book has helped hundreds of students and it can help you.

ATTENTION: ADULT LEARNERS

You may have fears of returning to school, but this book will help you become a successful student. Remember when you first learned to ride a bicycle? Even now when you get on the bike the skill returns. Learning skills are no different. Many of your skills may need polishing, and this can be done if you are determined to succeed. Perhaps you need extra help reprogramming negative thinking. If so, the following section on affirmations will help you.

AFFIRMATIONS

Affirmations are one way to lead your subconscious mind into helping you excel. Try saying these affirmations at least three times a day and posting them on your bathroom mirror or refrigerator to help you remember. They will work wonders in your life if you will simply try them. Use only one at a time depending on your special need that day.

- I AM AN EXCELLENT STUDENT AND DO WELL ON TESTS.

- I LEARN EASILY OR LEARNING IS EASY FOR ME.

- I AM A STRONG COMPETENT PERSON.

- I AM RELAXED AND READY TO LEARN.

- I CAN RECALL INFORMATION EASILY.

You may want to create your own affirmation, but be sure it is short and positive. Never use ''don't'' or ''not'' such as in ''I'm *not* stressed during a test.''

PART
II

TIME CONTROL

SAY ''NO'' TO YOURSELF

Learning to say ''NO'' to the voice inside your head that says ''I'm too tired to study'' or ''Let's party'' is absolutely necessary for academic success. This does not mean school must be a boring grind—it simply means that you must learn to control your time to insure there is room for both serious study *and* fun.

The following pages provide several time control tips, techniques and strategies. By following the ten ''Time Control Tips'' presented, you will be able to design your own flexible study schedule.

It is a good idea to carefully follow the schedule you complete for two or three weeks (making minor adjustments as needed) until it becomes routine. Remember there are such things as ''good habits'' too!

TIME CONTROL QUESTIONS AND TIPS

	CHECK WHEN COMPLETED	DATE

1. DO YOU HAVE A LARGE MONTHLY CALENDAR?

☐ _____

Write all important tests, deadlines, and activities on a large monthly calendar. Place it in a conspicuous location. Use color to highlight important dates— red dots or red pen.

2. DO YOU HAVE A WEEKLY APPOINTMENT CALENDAR?

☐ _____

Purchase one that shows a ''week-at-a-glance'' so you have a good overview of the entire week.

3. DO YOU HAVE A WEEKLY STUDY PLAN?

☐ _____

Use the blank weekly study schedule on page 15 to visualize and organize your time. Lightly pencil in your classes (by title on the days and times they meet) and block out times to eat, sleep, work, or study. Use this code (or one like it):

E = Exercise   **J** = Job
S = Study   **X** = Free Time
C = Commute   **Z** = Sleep

4. DO YOU PLAN FOR AT LEAST ONE HOUR OF STUDY FOR EACH CLASS PERIOD?

☐ _____

Protect time each day for study. By keeping a regular schedule, your study time will soon become habit forming.

5. DO YOU PLAN FOR STUDY BREAKS?

☐ _____

Remember to limit your straight study time to no longer than one hour. It is important to take a ten minute break between study periods to refresh yourself and give your mind a rest.

	CHECK WHEN COMPLETED	DATE
	☐	_____

6. **DO YOU PREVIEW TEXT ASSIGNMENTS AND REVIEW CLASSROOM NOTES FROM THE PREVIOUS CLASS BEFORE YOUR STUDY TIME?**

   Build this encoding strategy into your weekly schedule with ''P'' for preview and ''R'' for review. Add these items to your schedule.

7. **DO YOU MAKE EFFECTIVE USE OF ANY COMMUTE TIME TO SCHOOL EACH DAY?**

   If you travel to class and have an opportunity to do some schoolwork, this is an ideal time to preview or review. Place a ''C'' for all commute time on your schedule.

8. **DO YOU LEAVE SUFFICIENT TIME FOR RELAXATION AND PLAY?**

   Play is therapeutic. Without it you are only half a person. Make sure you have plenty of play time (marked with a ''P'') on your calendar. Meditation is a relaxing way to begin or end your busy day.

9. **DO YOU REWARD YOURSELF FOR MEETING GOALS?**

   No matter how tight your budget, you can always afford a date, a movie, an ice cream cone (or anything else that motivates you). Do not accept your reward if you do not meet your goal!

10. **ARE YOU A LIST MAKER?**

    It's a great idea to keep lists. Assign a priority to items on your list and try to complete the most important ones first. Carry forward items not completed on to your next day's/week's list.

LEARNING LADDER

RUNG 1: PRIORITIZE TIME

List five things you have to do
before tomorrow. Top priority items
are A; next in priority are B; less
urgent are C.

A, B,   **Mini-Priority List**
or C?

____ 1. _____
       _____
       _____

____ 2. _____
       _____
       _____

____ 3. _____
       _____
       _____

____ 4. _____
       _____
       _____

____ 5. _____
       _____
       _____

PRIORITIZE
TIME

Now label each item as an A, B, or C priority. Complete the ''A's'' first!

EXAMPLE OF A WEEKLY STUDY SCHEDULE

		MON	TUES	WED	THU	FRI	SAT	SUN	
6-7				BREAKFAST			WORK		
7-8			GET	READY FOR REVIEW	SCHOOL				
8-9		HIST.	CHEM.	HIST.	CHEM.	HIST.			
9-10		STUDY		STUDY		STUDY			
10-11			STUDY		STUDY			CHURCH	
11-12		FRENCH		FRENCH		FRENCH			
12-1					LUNCH				
1-2		MATH	WORK	MATH	STUDY	MATH	WORK	STUDY	
2-3		STUDY		STUDY	CHEM LAB	STUDY			
3-4									
4-5		ENG		ENG		ENG			
5-6		STUDY		STUDY	STUDY	STUDY			
6-7					DINNER				
7-8		STUDY	STUDY	STUDY	STUDY			STUDY	
8-9									
9-10									
10-11									

Exercise: 1. When do you plan for the next day or week? _____

2. When do you review your notes for the previous week? _____

3. How many times a week do you review the text or notes for a class? _____

4. Do you tape record lectures (with the instructor's permission) and listen in the car or when you are completing routine tasks? _____

BEGIN MAKING LISTS TODAY. COPY THIS PAGE AND USE IT
AS A MODEL FOR A WEEK, THEN ADAPT IT TO CREATE YOUR
OWN FORM. LIST MAKING SHOULD BECOME A HABIT.

DATE: _____

TODAY'S PRIORITY LIST

PRIORITY A, B, or C	SCHOOL	DONE
_____	1. _____	[ ]
_____	2. _____	[ ]
_____	3. _____	[ ]
_____	4. _____	[ ]
_____	5. _____	[ ]
_____	6. _____	[ ]
_____	7. _____	[ ]
_____	8. _____	[ ]
_____	9. _____	[ ]
_____	10. _____	[ ]

PERSONAL

_____	1. _____	[ ]
_____	2. _____	[ ]
_____	3. _____	[ ]
_____	4. _____	[ ]
_____	5. _____	[ ]
_____	6. _____	[ ]
_____	7. _____	[ ]

SUGGESTIONS: Be realistic. Plan to accomplish a few projects or errands each
day. As you complete an item, check it off. You may need to lower your
expectations and increase your performance. (Make copies for each day).

BLANK WEEKLY SCHEDULE

STOP! This blank weekly study schedule should be filled in by pencil at first. Your final schedule will probably not be completed until you have completed this program.

Look at the example on page 13 for guidance.

		MON	TUES	WED	THU	FRI	SAT	SUN	
6-7									
7-8									
8-9									
9-10									
10-11									
11-12									
12-1									
1-2									
2-3									
3-4									
4-5									
5-6									
6-7									
7-8									
8-9									
9-10									
10-11									

(This form may be copied without further permission from the publisher.)

P A R T
III

NOTETAKING
TECHNIQUES

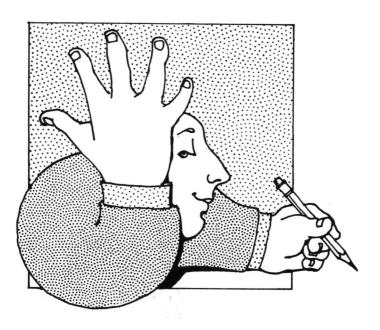

IMPORTANT NOTETAKING TECHNIQUES

Even if your instructor is a ''motor mouth,'' don't despair. Stay with it until you have learned the notetaking techniques presented on the next few pages.

---

1. Always read your assignment before you come to class. Otherwise, the lecture may sound as if it is in Greek. **BE PREPARED!**

2. Find a seat near the front of the room. Up close, you can see the board, be more aware of the instructor's facial expressions, hear better and not daydream or snooze as easily.

3. Identify some serious students in each class and get to know them. Get their phone numbers in case you have questions or need help during the term.

4. Copy everything the instructor writes on the board. This is especially true of examples, solutions, outlines, and definitions.

5. Organize and index your notes with colored tabs. If notes are allowed on any exam, you'll be ahead of the game.

WARNING!
DO NOT TRY TO WRITE DOWN EVERY WORD THE INSTRUCTOR SAYS. LISTEN FOR THE MAIN IDEAS. ABBREVIATE, OMIT, AND INVENT.

LEARNING LADDER

RUNG 2: SHARE IDEAS

As soon as possible get a phone number from a student in each of your classes. Your instructor can make this easier by asking who is willing to participate in a telephone exchange and then providing a master list of numbers.

Class   1. _____

Name   _____

Phone #   _____

Class   2. _____

Name   _____

Phone #   _____

Class   3. _____

Name   _____

Phone #   _____

Class   4. _____

Name   _____

Phone #   _____

Class   5. _____

Name   _____

Phone #   _____

SHARE IDEAS

PRIORITIZE TIME

EFFECTIVE LISTENING IS YOUR SECRET FOR BETTER CLASS NOTES

An outline format has been used below to refresh your memory on outlining skills.

I. Get Organized

    A. Use a spiral or 3-hole notebook to keep your notes organized. Avoid loose leaf folders that allow your papers to flutter everywhere.
Hint: Yellow paper may be easier on your eyes so consider changing from white to yellow.

    B. Date each lecture and number all pages for that course in sequence.

II. Set Up Your Format

    A. Study the sample notes on page 23. Use it, or experiment with something similar until you have a format you like.

    B. Recall words and abbreviations of main ideas should be written in the left margin of right hand page. Fill in recall words when you first review your notes. Study questions should be written on the facing left-hand page to assist you when you review.

    C. In your own words, summarize the main ideas at the bottom of the right hand page (or write questions you need to ask your instructor).

    D. Use an outline similar to the one on this page rather than writing full paragraphs.

        1. Indent secondary ideas, supporting documentation or examples.

        2. Always leave room when a new point is being developed.

        3. Incomplete sentences or phrases will be necessary. (Notice phrases used on the sample.) Make sure you know the meaning of all your incomplete sentences.

SECRETS FOR BETTER CLASS NOTES
(Continued)

III. **Taking Lecture Notes**

    A. What should you take notes on?

        1. All definitions

        2. Lists

        3. Formulas or solutions

    B. Indenting is important to set off secondary ideas. Leave plenty of space so the notes are easier to study.

    C. Draw arrows to show connections between ideas.

    D. Whenever you are in doubt, **write it down.** In discussion classes, jot notes on important points—particularly conclusions reached during the discussion.

    E. Spell new words as well as you can by the sound. Look up correct spelling the first chance you get, or ask your instructor for help.

    F. Use symbols, diagrams or drawings to simplify ideas.

IV. **Listening**

    A. Listen for the following signals from your instructor about what is important:

        1. Voice changes usually indicate important points—listen for increases in volume or dramatic pauses.

        2. Repetition is a clue that an important point is being made.

        3. Gestures may indicate a major point.

    B. Stay involved in all classroom discussions. Ask questions, especially when things are unclear.

V. **Participate in Class**

    A. Think, react, reflect, and question to help your instructor keep the class alive.

    B. Become involved but don't be a clown. Do not grandstand or dominate the conversation.

    C. Your grade will often improve if you actively participate. If you are on the borderline between grades, most instructors will remember your desire to learn if you participate.

SAMPLE NOTES

Use the recall cues on the "Classroom Notes" side to answer the study questions on the facing page. Write your answers on the lines provided.

STUDY NOTES & QUESTIONS OR TEXTBOOK NOTES		CLASSROOM NOTES MEMORIZATION STRATEGIES	
			9/27/86
		Recall	
		Cues	
		MEM?	I. Memory–types of
What are 2 types of memory:		LT	A. Long Term
[1]		ST	B. Short Term
[2]			
		GIM?	C. Strategies
What are 3 memory tips:		Mneu.	1. Mnemonics
[1]		S. Sent.	2. Silly Sentences
[2]		Vis.	3. Visualization
[3]			
		Use this space for:	
		1. Summary in your own words,	
		2. Questions, or	
		3. New Vocabulary	

Compare your answers with those of the author at the bottom of the page.

ANSWERS: (1) Long Term (2) Short Term (1) Mnemonics (2) Silly Sentences (3) Visualization

IMPROVE YOUR NOTETAKING

Speed writing can be increased by simplifying your handwriting.

- Write a sentence in your normal handwriting in the space below.

  _____

  _____

- Observe these inefficient notes with excessive loops, Now look at your sample (above) does it have any excessive loops? Notice how difficult they are to decipher.

  Notetaking is not the time for fancy writing.

- Simplify your handwriting; some printing may be necessary.

  Notetaking is the time to simplify. Change I to I.

REVIEW IMMEDIATELY!

Whenever possible, *spend 5-20 minutes* reviewing your notes immediately after class. Fill in missing areas and rewrite garbled notes. Studies show that short periods of study improve long term memory.

A TAPE RECORDER CAN BE AN ASSET, BUT DO NOT USE IT AS A CRUTCH OR SUBSTITUTE FOR TAKING NOTES!

IMPORTANT NOTETAKING ABBREVIATIONS

ABBREVIATE, OMIT, INVENT AND SIMPLIFY

COMMONLY USED ABBREVIATIONS:

>	increase	=	equals
<	decrease	ex.	example
∴	therefore	def.	definition
→	caused, led to	i.e.	that is
w/	with	vs.	versus
≠	unequal	bec.	because
w/o	without	≡	identical to
⊙	individual	imp.	important
sig.	significant	esp	especially

OMIT VOWELS:

mn = main
bkgd = background

unnec = unnecessary
ff = following

INVENT YOUR OWN ABBREVIATIONS COMMON TO YOUR DISCIPLINE:

subc = subconscious
sftwr = software
exst = existential
ct = computer terminal
chrm = chromosomes

Δ = change
Δ'ed = changed
Δing = changing
Δ'able = changeable

DO YOU USE OTHER ABBREVIATIONS? Add your own below:

_____

_____

_____

_____

LEARNING LADDER

RUNG 3: TAKE NOTES

HOMEWORK:

1. Take notes on a class lecture. Indent, use phrases, and review your notes by placing recall cues in the left hand margin.

2. After taking your notes, highlight the main points. Next, ask your instructor to evaluate the quality of the notes you took and make suggestions.

3. If you are working with a tutor, bring your notes to each meeting for review.

4. EXTRA CREDIT! Ask your instructor if you may complete assignments (such as turning in extra sets of notes) for additional credit.

NOTE:

Some Learning Resource Centers have videotapes of instructors which allow you to practice taking notes in a controlled setting.

P A R T

IV

CRITICAL
READING SKILLS

ormation as defined in subdivision (c) of Section 49061 which
district shall determine which individuals, officials, or orga:
irectory information, provided, however, that no informa
to a private profitmaking entity other than employers,
and representatives of the news media, including, but not
magazines, and radio and television stations. The nam
s enrolled in grade 12 or who have terminated enrollmer
may be provided to a private school or college operating

FIVE STEPS TO BETTER READING

Effective reading is probably the most important element of becoming a quality student.

Unfortunately, not everyone is blessed with good reading ability. Like any other skill, however, reading can be developed and improved with practice.

In the pages ahead, you will be introduced to a five step reading strategy that will help improve your reading skills by becoming a more critical reader.

THIS STRATEGY IS CALLED SQ3R.

TO LEARN MORE ABOUT IT . . .

CONTINUE READING.

SQ3R

SURVEY

QUESTION

READ & UNDERLINE

RECITE & WRITE

REVIEW

SQ3R FOR SUCCESS

When you read a love letter, you savor each word and have absolutely no difficulty concentrating. You do not need to underline the main ideas or make marginal notes. Textbook reading is different. You must learn to apply special reading and marking skills when you study complicated materials. An expansion of the SQ3R reading technique (explained below) can reduce your study time and significantly increase your ability to grasp essential information.

OVERVIEW OF SQ3R

Step 1: SURVEY

Step 2: QUESTION

Step 3: READ & UNDERLINE

Step 4: RECITE & WRITE

Step 5: REVIEW

STEP 1 | SURVEY

Spend no more than *10 minutes* to take a "sneak preview" of the reading you have been assigned. You may not be in the habit of previewing and will have to consciously force this important first step. *Previewing provides an overview of the way the chapter is organized.* Smart travelers use a road map and smart students survey first. You should:

- **Examine the title of each chapter.**
- **Note headings and subheadings and the relationship between the important headings in each chapter.**
- **Glance at diagrams, graphs or visuals.**
- **Quickly skim the introductory and concluding sections of each chapter.**
- **Notice any study questions or activities at the end of the chapter.**

STEP 2 | QUESTION

Begin with the first section of a chapter. Always read with the intent to answer a question. By using the words **who, what, when, where, why** or **how**, turn each heading into a question.

See if you can do this by writing two questions for Step 1 and Step 2: (Check below for the author's answer.)

1. _____

2. _____

STEP 3 | READ AND UNDERLINE

Read each section with the question you developed in mind. *After* reading the section, go back to the beginning and underline, highlight, and/or mark the material using the techniques discussed on pages 33 and 34.

Speed reading techniques should not be used for technical material because important details may be missed. Do not be afraid to move your lips or read aloud. It is a myth that rereading a sentence is harmful. Critical reading may require you to reread items several times to completely understand a sentence or passage.

1. "Why is surveying important," or "How do I survey a chapter?"
2. "How do I create questions from the heading of a section?"

STEP 3 READ AND UNDERLINE (Continued)

SUGGESTIONS FOR MARKING YOUR TEXTBOOK

> Use a ball point pen to mark your text because pencil fades. Purchase a highlighter to emphasize important information.

A. UNDERLINE AFTER READING

Read a paragraph or a section of the text and then *go back and underline only the main points.* Do not underline the first time you read the material.

B. USE NUMBERS FOR THE FOLLOWING:

Use numbers for:
1) lists
2) enumerations
3) sequences

C. VERTICAL LINES

Place **vertical lines** in the margin to emphasize main points of several lines.

D. ASTERISKS*

Use **asterisks** for main points and for other important points or ideas.

E. RECALL PHRASES

Place **recall** phrases in the margin to condense major points and provide supporting details. Summaries and questions may also be placed in the margin.

F. DEFINITIONS & EXAMPLES

Underline all definitions. Write ''def.'' in the margin. Put parentheses (   ) around examples. If you underline or highlight the entire example, your page will be a mass of yellow and your purpose for marking will be lost.

STEP 3 | READ AND UNDERLINE (Continued)

MARKING YOUR TEXTBOOK (Continued)

G. CIRCLES OR BOXES

Some students like to (**circle**) important concepts, ideas or subheadings.

Other students prefer a [**box**].

H. HIGHLIGHTING

Highlight the points underlined or highlight in place of underlining. Use a felt tip pen. Yellow is often preferred.

J. ??!!

React to what you read. Agree, disagree, question! Stay involved with the ideas in the text!

K. PRACTICE

Like any skill, practice is the best way to learn marking skills. Would you be confident that you could drive a car after simply listening to a lecture? Show your instructor a sample of your ''markings'' until you are confident you are selecting the most important material in each paragraph.

LEARNING LADDER

RUNG 4: READING SKILLS

<u>YOU TRY IT!</u>

Read the paragraphs on the following page, and then underline or highlight and add recall phrases in the left margin. To save time, underline and mark *only the second paragraph.*

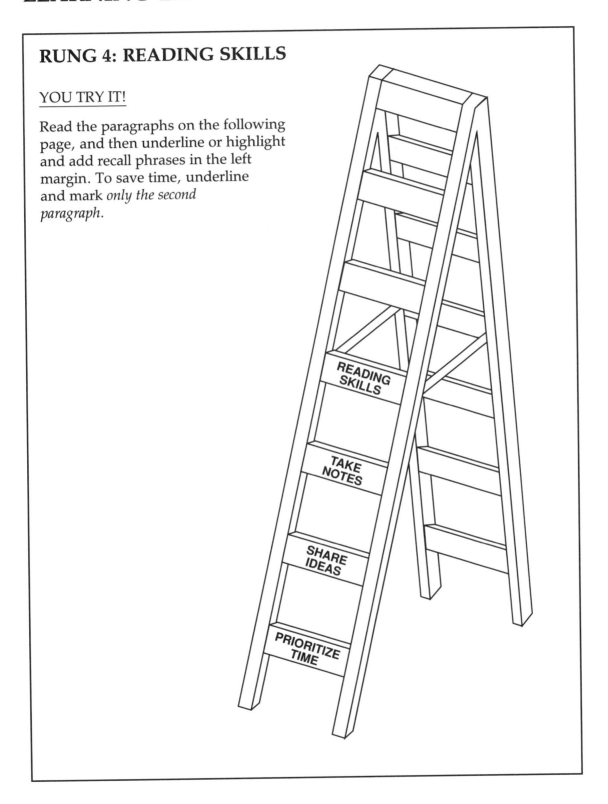

READING
SKILLS

TAKE
NOTES

SHARE
IDEAS

PRIORITIZE
TIME

STEP 3 | READ AND UNDERLINE (Continued)

ACADEMIC PRESSURE*

**RECALL
CUES**

Of course academic pressure is not applied evenly during the semester or quarter. There are times (especially during midterms and finals) when all your professors will expect special work from you at once. Themes will be due and examinations will be scheduled all within a few days. These demanding periods produce unusual pressure and strain, especially if you have made the mistake of getting behind in your work. The pace picks up, frustrations increase, fear takes a firmer grip, and students appear haggard and drained. It's a period of too much coffee, too many pills, and too little sleep—a desperate time with a touch of madness. Not only does it hurt your physical and mental health, but when the pressures force abnormal behavior, you can make foolish mistakes and jeopardize your academic progress.

**LOOK FOR
A TOPIC
SENTENCE.**

**READ WITH
A QUESTION
IN MIND**

How can you keep the peak period madness from hurting you? How can you avoid becoming too tense and frantic? Here are three suggestions: Stick as close as possible to your regular study and work schedule. Avoid late hours. Get some extra work done, but get enough sleep to avoid the tension merry-go-round that spins some students into a state of chaos. Avoid stimulants. Stay away from excessive coffee and drugs that keep you awake but destroy your ability to think clearly and logically when you need to. Assume an air of detachment from the whole crazy rat race. Look at it from a distance. Float through it with a calm head and confident manner. Watch the behavior of others who fall prey to the pressures, but refuse to become overinvolved yourself. But what if the pressure builds up too much despite your preventive measures? Is there a last-minute safety valve? Physical exercise is a good antidote. Jog. Play ball. Go bowling. Physical activity is one way to reduce stress resulting from a heavier-than-usual academic load.
(Con't. on page 37)

* Reprinted with the permission of the author, Elwood N. Chapman. *College Survival: A Do-It-Yourself Guide.*

STEP 3 READ AND UNDERLINE

COMPARE YOUR UNDERLINING AND MARGINAL
NOTATIONS WITH THE AUTHOR'S EXAMPLE BELOW.

ACADEMIC PRESSURE*

**RECALL
CUES**

Of course academic pressure is not applied evenly during the semester or quarter. There are times (especially during midterms and finals) when all your professors will expect special work from you at once. Themes will be due and examinations will be scheduled all within a few days. These demanding periods produce unusual pressure and strain, especially if you have made the mistake of getting behind in your work. The pace picks up, frustrations increase, fear takes a firmer grip, and students appear haggard and drained. It's a period of too much coffee, too many pills, and too little sleep—a desperate time with a touch of madness. Not only does it hurt your physical and mental health, but when the pressures force abnormal behavior, you can make foolish mistakes and jeopardize your academic progress.

1. Sleep.

**2. Avoid
    stimulants.**

3. Detachment.

**4. Physical
    Exercise.**

*How can you keep the peak period madness from hurting you? How can you avoid becoming too tense and frantic? Here are four suggestions: Stick as close as possible to your regular study and work schedule. Avoid late hours. Get some extra work done, but (1) get enough sleep to avoid the tension merry-go-round that spins some students into a state of chaos. (2) Avoid stimulants. Stay away from excessive coffee and drugs that keep you awake but destroy your ability to think clearly and logically when you need to. (3) Assume an air of detachment from the whole crazy rat race. Look at it from a distance. Float through it with a calm head and confident manner. Watch the behavior of others who fall prey to the pressures, but refuse to become overinvolved yourself. But what if the pressure builds up too much much despite your preventive measures? Is there a last-minute safety valve? (4) Physical exercise is a good antidote. (Jog, Play ball, Go bowling.) Physical activity is one way to reduce stress resulting from a heavier-than-usual academic load.

READING SKILLS (Continued)

STEP 4 RECITE & WRITE

Once you have formed questions on your reading and have read to answer those questions, you are ready to recite the answers. Use your underlining and markings to guide you. **Recite the answers out loud (or to yourself).** Also **write brief study notes** which will help encode the information in your long-term memory for easier retrieval on the final examination.

Write a sentence summary of the main idea in each paragraph if the material is extremely difficult for you.

The recall cues you wrote in the margins are an essential step. If you use those cues to recite, you may not need study notes in some classes.

STEP 5 REVIEW

Once you have read an entire chapter, section by section, you are ready to review that chapter.

This is the **final** step in understanding the material.

1. **Reread** each main heading.
2. **Review** the underlined and highlighted material.
3. **Answer** the questions you formed for each section. Use your reading notes to help you review.

LEARNING LADDER

RUNG 5: PRACTICE LESSON

After you finish steps three, four and
five select a chapter in one of your
textbooks and mark, highlight,
and make brief study notes
(1 to 1½ pages only). Then ask
your instructor or tutor to
review your notes with the
underlining and recall
cues in the margins,
and have that person
make suggestions
for improvement.

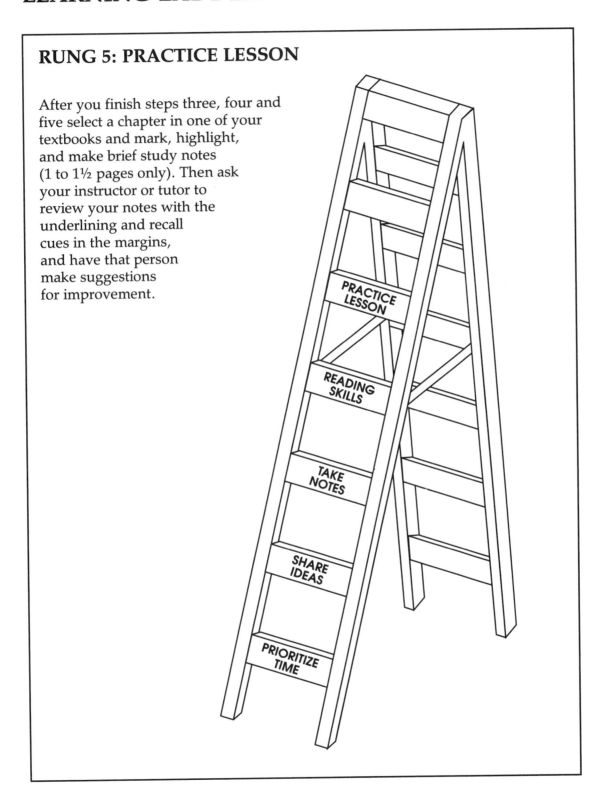

P A R T

V

MEMORY TRAINING

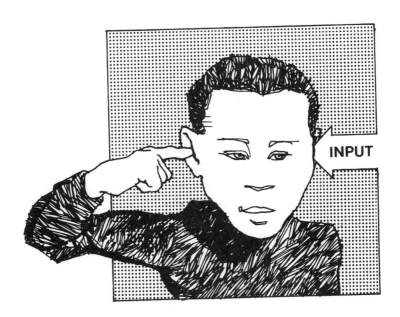

IMPROVE YOUR MEMORY

Human beings are capable of extraordinary feats of memory. In fact, experts in the study of memory agree that the skill was not all due to an inborn ability, but was developed through the use of various techniques and considerable practice.

Like the experts, you too can improve your memory. In the next few pages, several steps will be presented which, if learned and practiced, can make your studying not only easier—but more rewarding.

STEPS FOR MEMORY TRAINING

Have you studied for hours trying to memorize material for a test and then gone blank? To help you reduce blanking out, practice the following memory strategies. If test taking anxiety is severe, see your counselor or instructor for relaxation exercises.

OVERVIEW OF MEMORY TRAINING STEPS

- Spread your memory work over several sessions
- Recite material out loud
- Expect to remember (assume a positive attitude)
- Organize your material into a meaningful pattern
- Test and retest yourself
- Overlearn
- Use hooks, catchwords and rhyming phrases or sentences
- Study before sleeping

STEP 1 **SPREAD OUT** Memory Work

Sometimes students think that the longer they study, the more they will learn. Unfortunately, the reverse is true. Shorter periods of memory work—not more than two hours each—are far superior to six hours of frantic cramming.

REMEMBER!

REVIEWING MEMORY WORK WITHIN TWENTY-FOUR HOURS OF THE FIRST STUDY SESSION IS THE MOST EFFECTIVE WAY TO MASTER THE MATERIAL.

DISTRIBUTED PRACTICE

Probably the more time you spend studying the better, but *distributed practice* is the optimum strategy. An ideal learning pattern would involve:

1. Immediate review within the short term memory span.
2. A review after the first hour.
3. A short review after overnight sleeping.
4. A short review after a week.
5. A short review after a month.

Do you know how much more you will be able to recall if you follow this schedule? Up to 88% of the material you review will be saved in your long term memory.

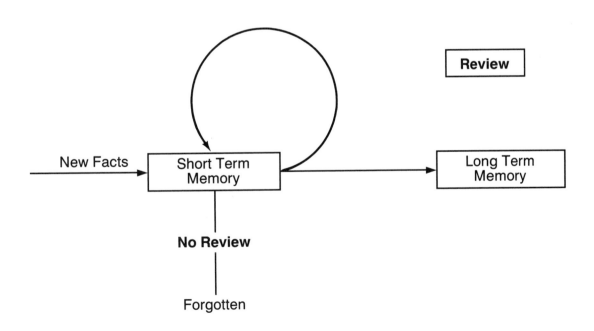

MEMORY TRAINING (Continued)

| STEP 2 | **RECITE** Material Aloud

When you are studying or memorizing, recite the answers to your study questions aloud so that you can hear the answer. Don't simply recite the answer in your head! That's a beginning, but *only* a beginning.

> **RESEARCH STUDIES SHOW THAT ANSWERING QUESTIONS ALOUD IMPROVES RECALL BY AT LEAST 80%!**

Question yourself aloud and answer yourself aloud.

If you study in a group or with a friend, quizzing each other will improve recall. Although your memory may begin to fail on a test, the voice of the person you studied with will often come through loudly and clearly.

USE ALL YOUR SENSES

The more senses you involve in the learning process, the longer you will remember.

See It　　**Read** and *visualize* the material.

Say It　　**Answer the questions** aloud that you formulate from your class notes. Use the cues in the recall column of your textbook and your notes to help you ask yourself study questions.

Write it　　**Write** answers to questions from your study notes. Outline major points from the text.

Repeat It　**Repeat** this entire process until you have mastered the material.

NEW RESEARCH

ALSO USE SMELL Study with a pleasant fragrance near you, such as a perfume or cologne, and take the test with the same fragrance nearby.

| STEP 3 | Expect to **REMEMBER** |

Make a *decision* to remember! As obvious as this seems, many students fail to realize the power of an intent to recall. Because you want to remember to a favorite song, you can easily repeat the lyrics word for word. If you *want* to remember, you will.

Your attitude is the secret. Believe in yourself and in your ability to learn.

| STEP 4 | **ORGANIZE** the Material |

People who recall long lists of numbers often can do so because they have found a *pattern or a relationship*.

Look at this string of numbers and take a moment to try to memorize the list.

3   6   9   12   15   18   21   24

a. What is the pattern in this string of numbers?
   Write your answer below.

_____

b. Do you see a pattern to these numbers?

6   13   19   24   28   31   33   34

Include no more than seven pieces of information in each organizational pattern. Cognitive psychologists have found that we retain no more than seven chunks of information best. Our telephone numbers (excluding area codes) are examples of the need to limit information to seven bits for better recall.

(Turn page upside down for answers.)

a. Increasing by 3 each time.   b. Increasing by 7, by 6, by 5, etc, in a regular sequence each time.

MEMORY TRAINING (Continued)

STEP 5   **TEST** and Retest Yourself

If you had to learn 10 definitions for class tomorrow, how could you test yourself? Would you write the definitions over and over or read the list aloud 20 times? Neither method is the **best** choice.

Instead, follow this self-testing process:

1. *Memorize the first* item.
2. Go on to the *second item* and memorize it.
3. Now *repeat* the *first item* and the *second* by memory.
4. When you know those two, *go to the third.*
5. *Memorize the third item* and *repeat items one, two,* and *three.*
6. *Continue* in this same manner until all 10 definitions have been learned.

DON'T FORGET TO USE
ALL YOUR SENSES:

READ IT!   **WRITE IT!**   **SAY IT!**

SING IT!   **IMAGINE IT!**

STEP 6   **OVERLEARN**

Review material that you have learned several times. When final examinations or midterms come around, you will have mastered material that you have encoded for long term recall. In math classes, rework the model or sample five or more times to encode the correct formula into your long term memory.

- Commercials can haunt you for years because of the *constant repetition* of a jingle or song. Can you complete this commercial?

  "Pizza!   Pizza!"

Answer: *Little Ceasar's*

| STEP 7 | **RECALL:** Use HOOKS, CATCHWORDS and RHYMING WORDS |

HOOKS
You hook the idea into your memory bank by using a *single letter* or *catchword* to pull up more information.

Most people have been taught ROY G. BIV to remember the colors of the rainbow.

Red   **O**range   **Y**ellow

Green

Blue   **I**ndigo   **V**iolet

CATCHWORDS
To remember these eight memory techniques, you can employ a similar hooking device.

S   **S**pread Out Memory Work
R   **R**ecite Aloud
E   **E**xpect to Remember
O   **O**rganize the Material
T   **T**est and Retest
O   **O**verlearn
R   **R**ecall with Hooks and Catchwords, etc.
S   **S**tudy Before Sleeping

If the *order* is *not important,* you can create a catchword or phrase from the *first letter* of the words. The strange or bizarre is usually easier to remember.

YOU TRY IT!   CREATE A WORD BY SCRAMBLING THE ABOVE LETTERS FROM THE LIST OF MEMORY TECHNIQUES. SPEND NO MORE THAN 5 MINUTES THINKING.

___ ___ ___ ___ ___ ___ ___ ___

(See author's suggested answer on page 50.)

MEMORY TRAINING (Continued)

| STEP 7 | (Continued) |

RHYMING

If words must be remembered in a specific order, then a rhyming nonsensical sentence may help you remember. When rhythm is added, the results are even better. We all know

> Thirty days hath September
> April, June, and November.

Notice that the poem rhymes and has rhythm.

| STEP 8 | **STUDY** Before Sleeping and Upon Awakening |

To get the most mileage from study and memory work, *you should review right before going to sleep.* Cut off the television and do not become otherwise distracted.

You will process this new material while you are sleeping. As you wake, review again. To put a tight cap on the bottle of information you are encoding for future recall, *review again* the same morning.

The author's suggested answer is the catch word ROOSTERS. Each letter is a signal for the first word of one of the eight memory techniques. If you want to remember even longer, *visualize* in your "mind's eye" or associate the catch word with an object or a place with which you are already familiar. Can you remember the image of roosters in a picture book from your childhood or even better, actual roosters that you have seen.

VISUALIZE

CAN YOU REMEMBER WHAT ROOSTERS STANDS FOR?
Refer back to Step 7 to help fill in the blanks.

R _____
O _____
O _____
S _____
T _____
E _____
R _____
S _____

VISUALIZE FOR SUCCESS

When you can visualize items from your text or classroom notes, they are much easier to recall. The rooster visualization was an example of how to use association to remember. Simpler visual patterns can be just as effective. *Whenever* possible use ''mind maps'' similar to the examples shown below to organize material (or create your own patterns). Once you've decided what information should be placed on your design, draw a new one and fill in the blanks from your memory.

SAMPLE PATTERNS

- **Chronological Time Lines** for History classes.

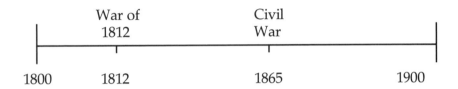

- **Trees** are popular among biology students and genealogists, but can be used for many academic subjects.

Try listing five skills you've learned from this book.

1. _____
2. _____
3. _____
4. _____
5. _____

Fill in this tree map using the five Rs on page 75.

- **Flow Chart** for Math classes

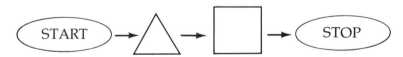

- **Study Map** for English classes

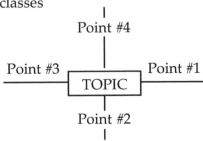

VISUALIZE FOR SUCCESS (Continued)

• **Sun Shapes or Clocks** for items that occur in a particular sequence.

• **Clustering or branching lines** for short essays.

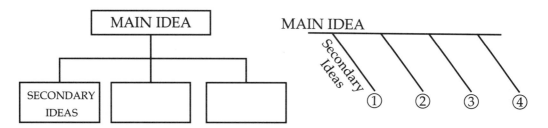

• **Hand Prints** for ideas of equal importance. Speeches can also be given with greater ease using the hand print. Do not use more than 10 items on each test to avoid confusion.

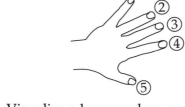

Visualize a key word on each finger.

• **Loci Method**

The ancient Greeks used the rooms of a house to help remember the points of a speech. You can do the same by walking through the front door and visualizing your introduction, into the living room for your first point and so on. The point is that we can link new information more easily on to a previous memory, like our homes or even parts of our car. Use whatever is the most vivid and familiar image to you as you apply the Loci method.

> ASSOCIATION IS AN IMPORTANT TECHNIQUE
> FOR EFFICIENT RECALL.

LEARNING LADDER

RUNG 6: MEMORY TECHNIQUES

LEARNING LADDERS

1. Map a chapter from a text or from a lecture in one of your classes using one or more of these techniques. Color will also create a stronger glue for your mind and is highly recommended by cognitive psychologists. Try it several times before giving up on the technique.

2. Pick one of the visual patterns to map 12 techniques covered in this section.

3. Consolidate the information on SQ3R using a handprint.

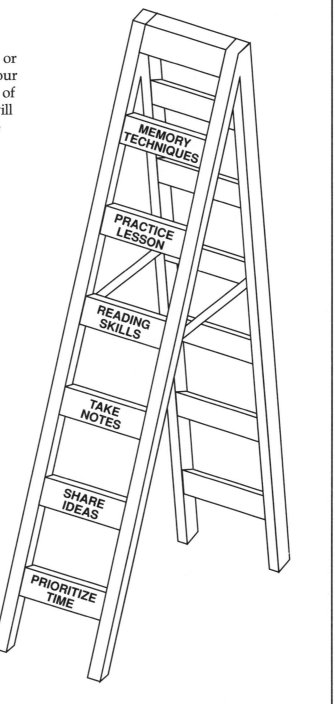

REVIEW OF MEMORY TECHNIQUES

A. THE EIGHT MEMORY STRATEGIES

   1. Spread memory work over several sessions

   2. Recite material out loud

   3. Expect to remember (assume a positive attitude)

   4. Organize the material into a meaningful pattern

   5. Test and retest yourself

   6. Overlearn

   7. Recall: use hooks, catchwords and rhyming

   8. Study before sleeping and upon awakening

B. VISUALIZE FOR SUCCESS

   1. Use chronological time lines to remember dates

   2. Sketch trees and fill in the branches with material to be learned

   3. Use flow charts to remember things in sequence

   4. Create a study map

   5. Make sun shapes or clocks to remember the relation on various items

   6. Cluster thoughts in an outline format

   7. When there are ten or fewer items to learn, use hand prints

   8. Use the Loci method

C. REVIEW THIS SECTION OF STUDY SKILLS STRATEGIES OFTEN

P A R T
VI

EXAM
STRATEGIES

TAKING TESTS WELL

Lynne was a typical student who faced a common challenge—three major tests and a final examination would account for 60% of her final grade. Often Lynne blanked out on exams and found it difficult to finish during the time allotted. If you have felt this test-taking anxiety, you are not alone.

Successful students, however, have learned some sound strategies for test taking. If you understand the sections presented earlier in this book on taking classroom notes, reading your textbook, and memory training, you are now ready to "**score**" by learning test-taking strategies.

Relaxation tapes and techniques can also be learned to reduce stress and can be an enormous help to you. Relaxation is crucial for optimum learning so try a few deep breaths before you begin to study. Some researchers have found that playing Baroque music is particularly helpful for learning at home or in the classroom. If Baroque music doesn't appeal to you, try something soothing and calming. This creates a linkage between the right and left brain and establishes an emotive link with the material.

**LEFT BRAIN
emphasizes:**

language

mathematical
   formulae

logic

numbers

sequence

linearity

analysis

words of a song

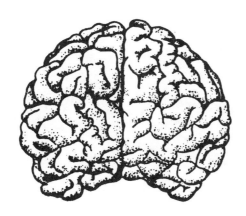

Corpus Callosum

**RIGHT BRAIN
emphasizes:**

forms and patterns

spatial manipulation

rhythm and
   musical appreciation

images/pictures

imagination

daydreaming

dimension

tune of a song

NO TEST-TAKING SECRET OR GIMMICK CAN SUBSTITUTE FOR THOROUGH PREPARATION!

TIPS FOR TAKING OBJECTIVE TESTS

To do well on an objective test, you need to memorize facts and thoroughly understand concepts and relationships. The following hints should help you score higher on true-false and matching type questions. Use your instructor as a resource. Ask him/her what type of questions will be on the test, and then prepare accordingly.

Some Hints:

- **Look over the entire test;** know how much each question is worth and budget your time accordingly. Check the clock every 10 minutes to insure you will not be caught off guard and run out of time. If necessary, put your watch on the desk in front of you.

- **Answer the easiest questions first.** Put a check by those that are harder and return to those questions last. Otherwise, you will waste valuable time and miss answering the easier questions. Place another line through the check when you complete the harder questions.

- **Underline key words in the question.** Make special note of negative words like ''not.'' Feel free, however, to ask for clarification from your instructor if the question is vague or unclear.

MATCHING QUESTIONS

Approach matching question testing as a game and play by the rules.

Rule # 1   As always, you begin by reading the question and underlining or numbering key words.

Rule # 2   Glance over both columns quickly. Which column has the longer entries? Begin looking at that side so you can save time as you scan the shorter column for an answer each time.

Rule # 3   Warning! Do not select an answer unless you are certain you've selected a correct match. Why? Because you've substantially reduced the number of items left for the more difficult final matches.

Rule # 4   Circle or draw a line through each answer that you eliminate.

Rule # 5   As you eliminate the matches you are sure of, use your best guess for the correct answer. It's OK to guess at this point.

TIPS FOR TAKING OBJECTIVE TESTS
(Continued)

TRUE-FALSE QUESTIONS

• Answers containing such words as *"all," "never," "always,"* and *"everyone"* usually are wrong.

• On the other hand, qualifiers like *"frequently," "probably,"* and *"generally"* more often indicate a true answer.

EXAMPLE

T   F   Class notes should *always* be rewritten.

The word "always" is a clue that the answer may be false.

MULTIPLE CHOICE QUESTIONS

1. *Draw a line through each answer which you eliminate.* (See example under #5 below.)

2. *Insure that the grammatical structure* of the question agrees with your choice.

3. *Read all choices.* Even if the first answer seems correct, another choice may be better, or "all of the above" may be the correct response.

4. *If you are at a complete loss, and there is no penalty for guessing, choose the longest answer*—especially on teacher-made exams.

5. When opposite statements appear in a question, one of the statements is often correct.

EXAMPLE

When two opposite statements appear in a multiple choice question

a) one of the opposite statements is usually correct.
b) ~~neither are correct~~.
c) ~~both are correct~~.
d) ~~choice in the middle is often correct~~.

ESSAY EXAMINATIONS

PREPARATION FOR ESSAY EXAMS

Do essay exams create more anxiety for you than objective exams? Fear of unknown essay questions can be substantially reduced if you follow these three simple steps:

Step 1: *Develop your own practice essay questions* by looking over your lecture notes and textbook assignments, and guessing what the instructor would select.

Step 2: *Sketch out a variety of outline responses* to 10 or more possible questions.

Step 3: *Memorize the outlines* using catch phrases or mnemonic (memory) devices.

Step 4: *Practice writing an essay* within a specific time constraint. This is especially helpful if you have difficulty completing your tests within the prescribed time.

Once you have reviewed and prepared for the test, you need to learn a few more skills that are particularly important on essay exams.

ESSAY WRITING SKILLS

Skill 1: *Read each question carefully and underline key words in the different parts of the question.* When you are asked to ''trace'' the development of social reform in America, you need to describe the historical development of the subject. On the other hand, when you are asked to ''criticize'' or ''critique'' a poem or book, your instructor expects you to show the positive and negative points and support your ideas with evidence.

CHECK YOUR KNOWLEDGE OF THE FOLLOWING FOUR WORDS, MOST OFTEN USED IN ESSAY QUESTIONS, BY FILLING IN THE BLANKS (Answers at bottom of page)

1. **''Compare''** means to show the _____ between something and ''contrast'' requires that you explain the _____ between things.

2. **''Justify''** means to give _____ for your ideas.

3. **''Enumerate''** simply means to _____ the main events or reasons.

4. **''Describe''** implies giving a _____ description of an event, etc.

1) similarities, differences   2) reasons   3) list   4) detailed

ESSAY WRITING SKILLS (Continued)

5. **"Evaluate"** requires that you give the _____ and negative points and your own _____ on the issue.

Other words you will need to understand include:

evalute	prove	illustrate
analyze	relate	diagram
delineate	state	discuss

If any are unfamiliar, look up their meaning in a dictionary.

Skill 2: Take a few minutes to analyze the entire test, and budget your time accordingly. Jot the time available in the margin of the test.

Skill 3: Before writing, create an informal outline of the main ideas and supporting detail. Some students use a cluster outline similar to the one illustrated.

CLUSTER OUTLINE

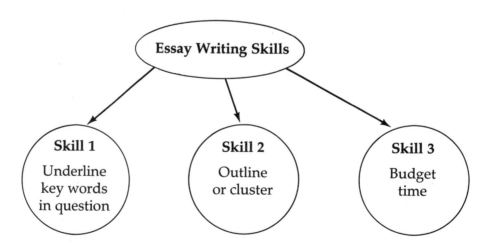

Essay Writing Skills

Skill 1
Underline key words in question

Skill 2
Outline or cluster

Skill 3
Budget time

5) positive   5) opinion

Skill 4: Strive for a well-organized, focused essay. The most common complaint from teachers is that essays they read are too general and do not provide adequate support for the ideas presented.

Avoid this problem by following the next three tips:

COMMON ERROR	HOW TO CORRECT IT
1. Padding	State your main point and stick to it. Avoid all extraneous material.
2. Weak Development	Develop three main points. Provide details, examples and/or statistics.
3. Choppiness	Use transition words similar to those shown on the following page to insure that your essay is more coherent. Transition words will show relationships between sentences and paragraphs.

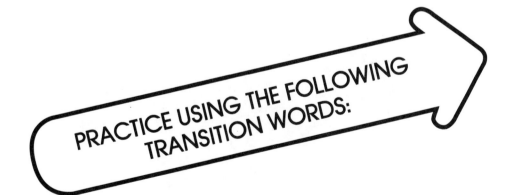

PRACTICE USING THE FOLLOWING TRANSITION WORDS:

TRANSITION WORDS

therefore	furthermore	consequently
moreover	of course	on the other hand
first	in conclusion	nevertheless
since	in addition	admittedly
also	finally	thus
first of all	next	assuredly

PRACTICE USING THE FOLLOWING TRANSITION WORDS!

Remember that these transition words can be used at the beginning of a sentence, in the middle, or at the end.

For example:

On the other hand, the brain only weighs three pounds.

The brain, on the other hand, only weighs three pounds.

The brain only weighs three pounds, on the other hand.

Using transitions makes your writing flow smoothly and shows relationships between sentences. Be sure to use them, but don't overdo it. Use no more than three in each paragraph, as a general rule.

Now write a paragraph of approximately five sentences using the information from the picture below. Incorporate at least one of the transition words from the above list.

YOUR BRAIN . . .

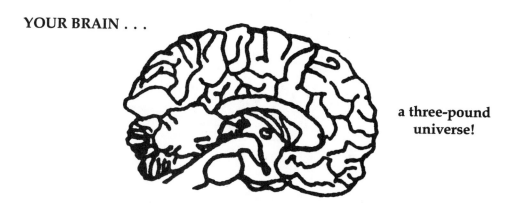

a three-pound
universe!

You have at least 100 billion nerve cells (neurons) in your brain.

Each of these neurons makes between 5,000 and 50,000 contacts with other neurons.

CLUSTERING

NOW YOU TRY IT!

Practice clustering by referring to Skill 4. Check your understanding on the following page.

ESSAY
QUESTION: *Describe three common errors* found in students' writing and *explain how to correct* those mistakes.

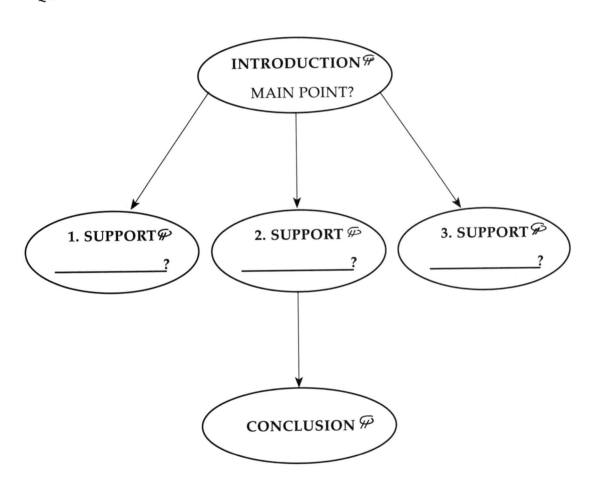

𝒫 = Paragraph

(Check your answers with that of the author on page 67.)

66

ESSAY EXAM MATCHING QUIZ

The following words are frequently used in essay examinations. Match the word to the appropriate definition.

1. ___ summarize

2. ___ evaluate

3. ___ contrast

4. ___ explain

5. ___ describe

6. ___ define

7. ___ compare

8. ___ discuss

9. ___ criticize

10. ___ justify

11. ___ trace

12. ___ interpret

13. ___ prove

14. ___ illustrate

A. show good reasons for

B. establish the truth of something by giving factual evidence or logical reasons

C. use a word picture, a diagram, a chart, or a concrete example to clarify a point

D. talk over; consider from various points of view

E. make plain; give your meaning of; translate

F. sum up; give the main points briefly

G. give an account of; tell about; give a word picture of

H. make clear; interpret; make plain; tell ''how'' to do

I. give the meaning of a word or concept; place it in the class to which it belongs and set it off from other items

J. bring out points of similarity and points of difference

K. bring out the points of difference

L. follow the course of; follow the trail of

M. state your opinion of the correctness or merit of an item or issue

N. give the good points and the bad ones; appraise

ANSWERS: 1. F, 2. N, 3. K, 4. H, 5. G, 6. I, 7. J, 8. D, 9. M, 10. A, 11. L, 12. E, 13. B, 14. C.

CHECK YOUR PROGRESS

ESSAY
QUESTION: *Describe the three common errors* found in students' writing and
explain how to correct those mistakes.

AUTHOR'S ANSWER

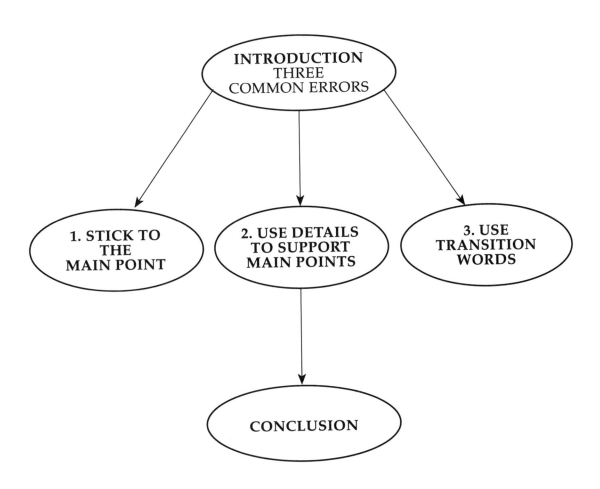

OTHER TIPS TO PREPARE FOR EXAMS

1. USE STUDY SHEETS

A study sheet has the questions on one page, and the answers on another as shown in the sample below.

QUESTIONS OR TERMS	TERMS
1. Explain eight memory techniques (ROOSTERS)	1. **R**ecite aloud.
	2. **O**rganize the material.
	3. **O**verlearn.
	4. **S**pread out memory work.
	5. **T**est and retest.
	6. **E**xpect to remember.
	7. **R**ely on the use of hooks, catchwords, etc.
	8. **S**tudy before sleeping.
2. Why recite answers out loud?	2. If you can retrieve information (recall) you have excellent control over the material. Long term memory is improved by 80%.

USING THE STUDY SHEETS

- After writing or reciting answers to the questions several times, you are ready to **fold the page** as shown below to cover the answers.

- If you can answer the question correctly, without looking at the answer, place a (✔) by the question.

- If you **cannot recall** the answer, **use the back side** of the paper to rewrite your response.

> 1. Explain 8 memory techniques (ROOSTERS)
>
> 2. Why recite answers out loud?

REPEAT THIS PROCESS UNTIL YOU HAVE MASTERED THE MATERIAL.

2. USE STUDY CARDS

Some students use 3 × 5 index cards to help them study. Cards may be used for mathematics, science, English, history—almost any academic subject.

FLASH CARDS ARE ESPECIALLY EFFECTIVE WHEN YOU ARE STUDYING A FOREIGN LANGUAGE OR ESL.

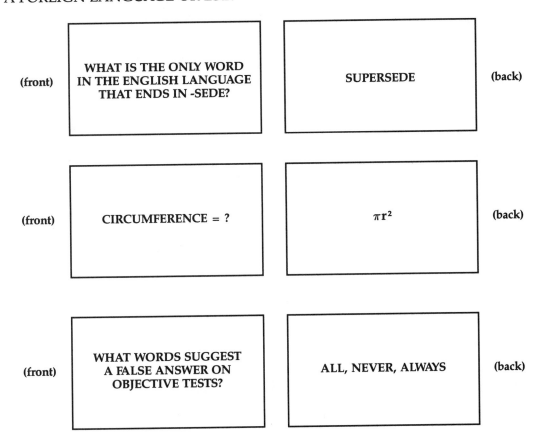

(front)   **WHAT IS THE ONLY WORD IN THE ENGLISH LANGUAGE THAT ENDS IN -SEDE?**   **SUPERSEDE**   (back)

(front)   **CIRCUMFERENCE = ?** πr^2 (back)

(front)   **WHAT WORDS SUGGEST A FALSE ANSWER ON OBJECTIVE TESTS?**   **ALL, NEVER, ALWAYS**   (back)

STEP 1: Look at the front side of the card and ask yourself the question.

STEP 2: Answer the question or define the concept. Then turn the card over to see if you are correct.

STEP 3: Correct? Place the card in a stack to your left.

STEP 4: Incorrect? Test and retest 3 times. Put that card in a stack to your right.

STEP 5: Have someone else ask you the questions repeating Steps 2 through 4.

EXAM STRATEGIES REVIEW

(CHECK THOSE YOU PLAN TO PRACTICE)

FOR OBJECTIVE TESTS:

☐ Answer easiest questions first.

☐ Underline key words in each question.

☐ Cross out items you have answered.

☐ Be alert for words such as ''always'' and ''never.''

☐ Insure that the grammatical structure of the answer is consistent with the question.

☐ If there is no penalty for guessing, answer every question.

FOR ESSAY EXAMS:

☐ Anticipate questions the instructor might ask.

☐ Sketch a variety of outline responses to model questions.

☐ Practice writing sample essays.

☐ Read each question carefully and underline key words.

☐ Analyze the entire test before beginning to write.

☐ Create an informal ''cluster'' outline of your response before starting to write.

☐ Strive for a focused essay, tightly organized and supported with facts.

VII

MATHEMATICS STUDY SKILLS

MATH TIPS, TECHNIQUES AND IDEAS

Mathematics requires special study skill techniques. This brief section will provide a few tips and ideas which should make your math study skills more effective.

Because math can be confusing, it will sometimes be necessary to ask for special help. If you become confused or lost, seek the assistance of your instructor or a tutor. Mathematics often builds on a set of rules, and if basic principals are not understood, the likelihood is that you will stay lost.

MATH STUDY SKILLS TIPS

| **Tip 1** | Because it is difficult to take notes on the instructor's explanation and copy the problem off the board, you may want to tape record the instructor's explanation. |

| **Tip 2** | Copy all the theorems, principles, and definitions *exactly*. Do not paraphrase or condense anything that is written on the board. *Also* be sure to copy the instructor's explanation. Draw arrows to the instructor's explanation for each step of the problem. |

| **Tip 3** | Rewrite math notes each day in ink for clarity and permanence. *Neatness* is especially important because of the need for accuracy. |

| **Tip 4** | *Rework model problems* over and over until you can do them without stopping. This is the crucial step that most students overlook. Instead of figuring out what is being taught in the model problem, they jump right into doing homework, and end up reworking problems several times. |

| **Tip 5** | Plan to work *at least two hours* on math homework for every hour of class time. Since you may need to spend ten to twelve hours working on math class assignments, set your priorities carefully and take a lighter academic load if possible. |

| **Tip 6** | Learn the five R's of math shown on the next page. |

THE FIVE R's OF MATH

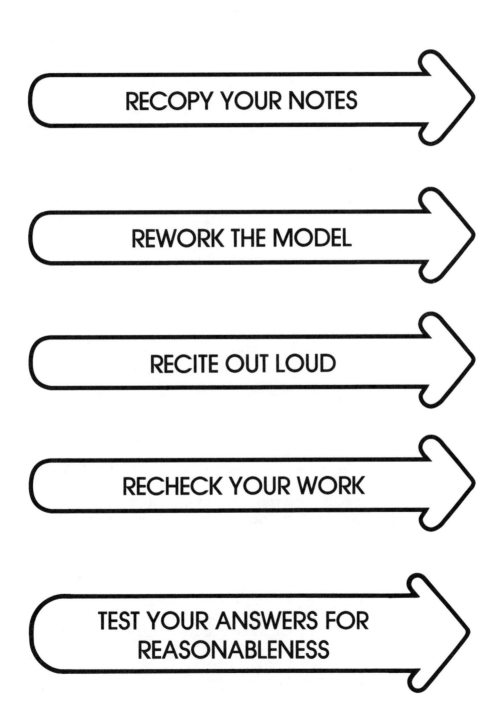

RECOPY YOUR NOTES

REWORK THE MODEL

RECITE OUT LOUD

RECHECK YOUR WORK

TEST YOUR ANSWERS FOR REASONABLENESS

PLAN OF ATTACK

To help you get an overview of the best math study skills, read the following Five R's for Math and write marginal notations or recall cues to the left of R1, R2, R3, R4, and R5.

RECALL
CUES

| THE FIVE R's OF MATH |

————
———— R_1 **Recopy** your notes in pen. Color code definitions, rules and problem areas discussed by your instructor. Neatness and legibility are your first steps toward becoming a better math student.
————

> How do you rate your math notes?
> ☐ Organized and clear
> ☐ Messy
> ☐ Disorganized but neat

————
———— R_2 **Rework** the model or example over and over until it can be done without hesitation.
————

> Have you ever taken this step before beginning your homework?
> ☐ YES   ☐ NO
> If not, try it for a week and see if it makes a difference.

————
———— R_3 **Recite.** Oral recitation is one more technique for improving your mathematical skills. Practice this step with a study partner or friend. Force each other to explain out loud each step of the process. In case you are studying alone, still express your thinking aloud.
————

> Have you ever used this oral recitation technique when you were studying math?
> ☐ YES   ☐ NO
> (Problem solving out loud is no longer the sign of senility but the mark of a critical thinker.)

RECALL
CUES

———————

——————— R_4 **Recheck** your computations. Also recheck your thinking process. This is even more important when you move from one step of a problem to the next, or from one concept to a new one.

———————

"MINDCHATTER" *

When the internal thinking of professionals was questioned and recorded by Dr. Arthur Whimbey and Dr. Jack Lochhead, a typical dialogue was similar to the following:

1. "Let me read the question again to be sure what's being asked. I'll circle or underline the question."

2. "Okay. I see, but I'll read it again to be sure."

3. "Slow down. Don't rush."

4. "What is given? What is known?"

5. "How can I diagram, make a chart, or draw a visual to help me?"

In all cases, lawyers, doctors, engineers, etc., were painstakingly careful to reread phrases and double check their work.

———————

——————— R_5 Test for **reasonableness.** Plug your answer into the problem to see if it makes sense. This final check could save you both time and embarassment later.

———————

Asking questions about how reasonable an answer is will make critical thinking a habit and problem solving less ominous.

---

* Adapted from Problem Solving and Comprehension, 4/e Whimbey and Lochead, Lawrence Erlbaum Associates, 1986.

MATH STRATEGIES REVIEW

MATH STUDY SKILL TIPS

- Copy all theorems, principles and definitions carefully and exactly.

- Rewrite math notes in ink — be neat.

- Rework model problems until they become second nature.

- Spend two hours working on homework for each hour of class time.

THE FIVE R's OF MATH

- R_1 – Recopy your notes.

- R_2 – Rework model problems.

- R_3 – Recite aloud to explain each step of the problem solving process.

- R_4 – Recheck your work.

- R_5 – Test your answers for reasonableness — insure your answer makes sense.

REMEMBER. . .If you are confused, do not wait to get help. The longer you are lost, the more likely you'll stay lost!

PART

VIII

FINAL COACHING REVIEW

LEARNING LADDER

RUNG 7: REVIEW SKILLS

DAY 1 **Discipline Your Time!** Make a revised time schedule using the blank on page 15. Place this schedule in your notebook and above your desk. Use it for two or three weeks, but modify it as necessary. You are in charge of all changes, and should allow yourself *some* flexibility.

DAY 2 Take class notes using the model format on page 23. Create study questions and highlight your notes today. Review for 5-10 minutes as soon as possible after each class. Also, review all the abbreviations and begin using them.

DAY 3 **Don't Stop Now!** Return to the Reading Skills Section beginning on page 27. Apply the SQ3R techniques to this book. The book is yours so mark it like you would any other text.

DAY 4 **Be Persistent!** Apply your study skills to a magazine article or any other material you want to study critically.

DAY 5 Take 30 minutes to review the entire Memory Section and memorize the concepts of learning signaled by the catchword ROOSTERS. Use this principle for one of your classes.

DAY 6 Take 30 minutes to memorize the hints for taking objective examinations. *You can do it!* Create a catchword or rhyming phrase of your own. Remember to recite aloud or study with another person.

DAY 7 CONGRATULATIONS! You are an excellent candidate for success because you are applying a plan of action that can become a pattern of learning for a lifetime.

REVIEW SKILLS

MEMORY TECHNIQUES

PRACTICE LESSON

READING SKILLS

TAKE NOTES

SHARE IDEAS

PRIORITIZE TIME

ON YOUR OWN

CONGRATULATIONS! You have now completed this short intensive study skills program. Your score in the review quiz on the following page will indicate the progress you have made in a very short period of time.

How can you continue to make progress? How can you learn to be a skillful student as well as a critical thinker? How can you use this information to improve your G.P.A.?

Follow the plan below and apply your skills. To begin, you may want to sign the voluntary contract in Appendix I with a teacher, counselor or friend to help you stay motivated.

FINAL REVIEW QUIZ

CHOOSE THE BEST POSSIBLE MULTIPLE CHOICE, FILL IN THE BLANK, OR TRUE/FALSE ANSWER.

_____ 1. Notes should be reviewed within
   a) 72 hours
   b) 24 hours
   c) 48 hours
   d) none of the above

_____ 2. When two opposite statements appear in a multiple choice question
   a) one of the opposite statements is usually correct
   b) neither are correct
   c) both are correct
   d) choice in the middle is often correct.

_____ 3. Recall cues are placed in the _____ margin of the paper.

_____ 4. Reciting answers to study questions improves memory by
   a) 82%
   b) 95%
   c) 70%
   d) none of the above.

T F 5. Study time should be divided into blocks of three to four hours.

T F 6. All notes should be rewritten or typed except for math notes.

T F 7. Visual organizers are best suited for art classes.

T F 8. "Mind Chatter" is "internal dialogue" used by professional problem solvers to find solutions.

T F 9. Read through a paragraph before you underline or highlight.

T F 10. SQ3R is a reading strategy developed for surveying and skimming easy material.

CHECK ANSWERS ON PAGE 84.

PLACE YOUR SCORE IN HERE

Each question is worth 10 points so if you miss two you earned 80/100 or 80%. If you scored less than 70% review the appropriate section of this book with more focused attention.

ANSWERS TO FINAL REVIEW

TIP: SAVE ALL OLD TESTS FOR REVIEW FOR
MIDTERMS AND FINAL EXAMINATIONS.

CHECK YOUR PROGRESS: Read carefully the explanation on questions
that you missed.

QUESTION	ANSWER	EXPLANATION
1.	B	Review classnotes as soon as possible, certainly within twenty-four hours so that abbreviations and garbled notes can be clarified.
2.	A	Often one of two opposite statements is correct in a multiple choice question.
3.	Left	Recall cues are placed on the left side on the margin.
4.	D	''None of the above'' was correct; 80% is the actual answer.
5.	F	Study time is best broken into 1 and 1½ hour intervals with ten minute breaks.
6.	F	Instead of recopying notes, study time is better spent writing study questions, recall phrases, and reciting answers out loud. Math notes however should be recopied.
7.	F	Visual organizers like trees, maps, etc., can be used in any subject.
8.	T	Professional problem solvers think methodically and ''talk'' themselves through the problem.
9.	T	To avoid too much underlining, read a paragraph first and then underline the important points when you reread it.
10.	F	SQ3R is used when reading difficult or complex material.

APPENDIX I

LEARNING CONTRACT

A definition of ACCOUNTABILITY is to be responsible for one's actions.

We all have good intentions. The thing that separates those who are successful from those who are not is how well these good intentions are carried out.

A Voluntary Contract (or Agreement) can help convert your good intentions into action.

The Voluntary Learning Contract on the facing page is a good starting point if you are serious about getting the most from your studies.

This Agreement can be initiated by either you, your advisor or instructor.

ENTER A LEARNING CONTRACT

APPENDIX I (Continued)

VOLUNTARY

LEARNING CONTRACT*

I, _____ , agree
(Student's name)

to meet with the individual designated below at the times
shown to discuss my study skills progress. The purpose of all
sessions will be to *review* study skills and establish action steps
in areas where improvement may still be required.

I agree to meet with the above individual on:
(Tutor, instructor, etc.)

_____

_____

_____
(describe schedule giving date and times)

_____
Signature (tutor, instructor, learning strategies leader, friend, coach, peer counselor)

Areas needing attention:

☐ Time Control
☐ Notetaking
☐ Power Reading
☐ Memorization Techniques
☐ Problem Solving (critical thinking)
☐ Career Goals
☐ Other _____

_____
Student's Signature   *Date*

*To The Instructor: Establishing personal contact with the student is
a critical step. The first conference should occur as early as possible
in the term. Some students may need to see you on a regular basis.

| APPENDIX II | **CHECKLIST FOR TUTOR/INSTRUCTOR** |

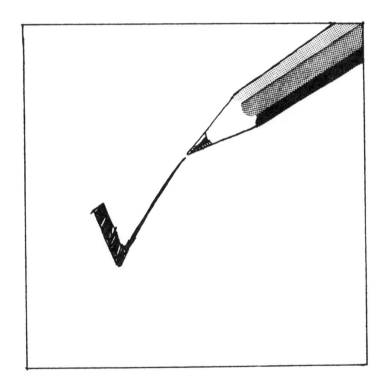

88

FOR THE TUTOR/INSTRUCTOR

New instructors and tutors need to be sensitized to potential learning problems experienced by students. The following checklist of questions will help alert the instructor/tutor to problem areas. Once these problem areas have been identified, a student should work through sections of *Study Skills Strategies* and/or other resources provided by the resource center. This checklist will help an instructor/tutor discuss progress with a student.

CHECKLIST FOR TUTOR/INSTRUCTOR

Tutor/Instructor: _____   Student: _____

Subject: _____

YES	NO		ACTION NEEDED
		Time Management	
_____	_____	1. Did I request a weekly time schedule during the first tutorial session?	_____
_____	_____	2. Do I have a copy of my student's course syllabus indicating course requirements, deadlines for papers, midterms, and finals?	_____
_____	_____	3. Have I helped my student set some short-term goals?	_____
		Notetaking	
_____	_____	1. Have I looked at the student's notes and identified strengths and weaknesses?	_____
_____	_____	2. Have I reviewed the model for recall cues and explained how to use these cues for studying?	_____
_____	_____	3. Have I asked my student to answer questions or find solutions to problems from a lecture using his/her notes to prompt me?	_____
_____	_____	4. Have I related lecture notes to textbook or other reading assignments?	_____
_____	_____	5. Does the student know different techniques to study his/her notes?	_____

YES   NO   ACTION
                                                                    NEEDED

Critical Reading Skills

_____   _____   1. Have I examined the methods used by my   _____
                     student to mark his/her textbook?

_____   _____   2. Have I asked if my student reads   _____
                     assignments prior to class?

_____   _____   3. Does the student know the value of the   _____
                     SQ3R method; and if so, is he/she using it?
                     If not, why?

SQ3R

SURVEY

_____   _____   1. Does the student know how to survey the   _____
                     entire chapter before reading the
                     assignment?

_____   _____   2. Does the student ask and/or write questions   _____
                     about the text as he/she surveys?

QUESTION

_____   _____   3. Does the student read for answers to   _____
                     his/her questions?

_____   _____   4. Does the student list questions he/she does   _____
                     not understand after reading
                     the text?

_____   _____   5. Does the student attempt to answer   _____
                     all questions before going to the next
                     textbook topic, section, or chapter?

READ & UNDERLINE

_____   _____   6. Does the student focus on the readings   _____
                     thoroughly and carefully and highlight key
                     concepts?

_____   _____   7. Can the student identify the topic sentences   _____
                     in a paragraph?

_____   _____   8. Have I explained how and when to use a   _____
                     multi-highlighter for a specific purpose
                     (e.g., vocabulary, main ideas, etc.)?

YES	NO		ACTION NEEDED

_____ _____ 9. Have I explained how to use special markings or symbols to identify important points or organization? _____

_____ _____ 10. Does my student understand how to reduce a chapter by outlining/overlining or visually organizing the material with flow charts, etc.? _____

RECITE & WRITE

_____ _____ 11. Does my student understand recitation and its relevance to recall and long-term memory? _____

_____ _____ 12. Does my student write out questions he/she does not understand or cannot answer? _____

REVIEW

_____ _____ 13. Does my student review? If so, how? _____

_____ _____ 14. Does my student write study notes? _____

Memory Training

_____ _____ 1. Does my student draw diagrams or visuals to better understand the problem? _____

_____ _____ 2. Does the student read through an entire problem before trying to solve it? _____

_____ _____ 3. Does the student work through a problem systematically, one step at a time? _____

_____ _____ 4. Does my student write or recite his/her reasoning used in each step of problem solving, including any assumptions made? _____

Exam Strategies

_____ _____ 1. Does my student review each test question prior to attempting to answer it? _____

_____ _____ 2. Is my student overly anxious about test taking? If so, have I suggested relaxation exercises? _____

_____ _____ 3. Does the student budget time wisely while taking an exam? _____

_____ _____ 4. Does the student answer easy questions first and go back through the exam to answer the more difficult questions last? _____

_____ _____ 5. Does the student understand how to identify key words in exam directions, and does my student know how to ''cluster'' in preparation for writing an essay? _____

NOTES

NOTES

NOTES

NOTES

OVER 150 BOOKS AND 35 VIDEOS AVAILABLE IN THE 50-MINUTE SERIES

We hope you enjoyed this book. If so, we have good news for you. This title is part of the best-selling *50-MINUTE*™ *Series* of books. All *Series* books are similar in size and identical in price. Many are supported with training videos.

To order *50-MINUTE* Books and Videos or request a free catalog, contact your local distributor or Crisp Publications, Inc., 1200 Hamilton Court, Menlo Park, CA 94025. Our toll-free number is (800) 442-7477.

50-Minute Series Books and Videos Subject Areas . . .

Management
Training
Human Resources
Customer Service and Sales Training
Communications
Small Business and Financial Planning
Creativity
Personal Development
Wellness
Adult Literacy and Learning
Career, Retirement and Life Planning

Other titles available from Crisp Publications in these categories

Crisp Computer Series
The Crisp Small Business & Entrepreneurship Series
Quick Read Series
Management
Personal Development
Retirement Planning